DAMNED THROUGH THE CHURCH

DAMNED THROUGH THE CHURCH

John Warwick Montgomery

BETHANY FELLOWSHIP, INC.
Minneapolis, Minn. 55438

Bethany Fellowship, Inc.
6820 Auto Club Road
Minneapolis, Minnesota 55438

Printed in U.S.A.

PREFACE

I take this opportunity to thank the Faith and Life Committee of the Evangelical Lutheran Synod of Eastern Canada for inviting me to deliver this lecture series at their Elim Lodge Retreat held September 7-9, 1962. I am particularly grateful that the men who were in attendance refused to quench the Holy Spirit of God as He led the speaker to prescribe strong medicine for the church in our day.

A special word of thanks is due to Pastor Wallace G. Minke of Good Shepherd Lutheran Church, Toronto, for his thoroughly evangelical Bible studies and for his dynamic Sunday sermon at Elim; and to Mr. Samuel Weicker of Kitchener, who faithfully transcribed my lecture-discussions from tape recordings made *in situ*. Readers of this book should keep in mind that it has its source in tape-recorded messages; the lecturer hopes that any departures from accepted literary style will be compensated for by a retention of the sense of immediacy which prevailed at Elim.

John Warwick Montgomery

All Saints' Day, 1969

CONTENTS

"And to the angel of the church in Laodicea write: 'The words of the Amen, the faithful and true witness, the beginning of God's creation.

" 'I know your works: you are neither cold nor hot. Would that you were cold or hot! So, because you are lukewarm, and neither cold nor hot, I will spew you out of my mouth. For you say, I am rich, I have prospered, and I need nothing; not knowing that you are wretched, pitiable, poor, blind, and naked. Therefore I counsel you to buy from me gold refined by fire, that you may be rich, and white garments to clothe you and to keep the shame of your nakedness from being seen, and salve to anoint your eyes, that you may see. Those whom I love, I reprove and chasten; so be zealous and repent. Behold, I stand at the door and knock; if any one hears my voice and opens the door, I will come in to him and eat with him, and he with me. He who conquers, I will grant him to sit with me on my throne, as I myself conquered and sat down with my Father on his throne. He who has an ear, let him hear what the Spirit says to the churches.' "

—Revelation 3:14-22

CHAPTER ONE

Why Do People Go to Church?

The subject of this book is "DAMNED THROUGH THE CHURCH." Now you may think that this is a severe title, but it is not half as severe as it was intended to be. When I was preparing this material in lecture form, I had originally intended to use the title, "Going to Hell through the Church"; but when I heard the quivering voice of the Retreat director on a long-distance phone call and realized that he would require medical attention if I used this title, I found it necessary to employ a more moderate expression.

I want to make very clear from the outset exactly what I mean by the title, "DAMNED THROUGH THE CHURCH." Today the word "damned" is used in a very loose way. Probably you realize that the old Will Hayes Production Code of film morality is no longer in operation. It used to be that when Bugs Bunny dropped a hammer on his foot he would say "ouch," but if you go to the movies today and Bugs Bunny drops a hammer on his foot he will be likely to yell "damn"; and there are no censors that will prevent this from happening. Today the word "damned" is used in a very loose way, often suggesting no more than strong disapproval of what has happened to us. But in this book I shall employ this term in the technical, theological sense of "eternally condemned."

You notice that in the title I have connected this negative term "damned" with one of the most positive terms that we have in the Christian faith, the church—a positive term and a negative term juxtaposed. And I haven't just put these side by side; I have *united* them: "Damned *through* the Church." This is to indicate that damnation and the church are not necessarily opposite—that it is not necessarily the case that a person in the church cannot be damned, or the person that is outside the church can't be saved—that these two terms are not mutually exclusive. I think that we are going to discover that the church and damnation often have a very close relationship. And we will have to ask ourselves: "Are damnation and the church connected in my own life?"

We are concerned first of all with the church, and I am going to begin with the simplest definition of it, the definition that you yourself would probably give if asked, namely, that a church is a local community of worship. When the term is used today, this is what is ordinarily meant by it. A church is a local community of worship, that is, the place where you go to worship with your friends and acquaintances.

What we want to discover at the very outset is why people go to church at all. Now we could ask a pastor, but this would not be a very successful way of getting at the problem because a pastor would probably not indicate to us why people *do* go to church but why people *should* go to church. What we need is a statement from a layman, a person who is not self-consciously speaking in behalf of the church. Fortunately we have such a lay statement in an article by the late journalist Stanley High. Stanley High was a writer especially interested in religious subjects. Indeed, one of his last books was a biography of Billy Graham. (Let me say, parenthetically, that I have the highest respect for Billy Graham; would that more pastors preached as biblically straightforward sermons as he does. I will oppose virtually all negative evaluations of Graham. But note that high praise for Graham is not necessarily to praise High!) In 1937, over thirty years ago, the *Saturday Evening Post* ran an article by Stanley High entitled, "I go to Church." The *Reader's Digest* subsequently condensed this and published it twice because it so well spoke the language of the churchgoer of the present time. Let us see if we can discover High's reasons for going to church. We shall use two criteria in interpreting the article: first, we must understand what it says before we begin to criticize it, and secondly, we must recognize that the article cannot be *completely* good or *completely* bad (since neither God nor the devil wrote it, but only Stanley High!).

I have sat in my quota of hard pews, heard my share of "volunteer" choirs and listened to enough uninspired and uninspiring sermons to last a lifetime. But I still go to church. I go to the church at the end of the street in the little town where I live.

I was raised a Methodist and at one time was a Congregationalist. The church at the end of the street happens to be Presbyterian. My wife belongs to the guild. We both like the preacher. It is convenient. But it lays claim to no special distinction. We have good music but it is no better than the Sunday-morning music I could get on the radio. The preacher is better than average. But his renown is pretty much limited to our town.

My church, in short, is like 10,000 other small-town churches, with no more to offer, and no less. But I enjoy it. I feel that I have missed something when I do not go.

I grant that habit may have something to do with it. My Methodist parents laid great store by churchgoing, and so, as a boy, did I. It would be difficult to shake the influence of that early training. About half past ten on Sunday mornings, the old youth-bred inclination lays hold of me. If I stay at home, I do it in the face of an internal protest. I suppose if I stayed home often enough I would get over that feeling. But I generally go.

I go to church for the same reason that I go to the theater—because I get something out of it. What I get is different. But it is something that I want and I have not found any other place where I can get it.

For one thing, at church I generally get some perspective—often not so much as I would like, but always a little. That little is more than I can be sure of getting anywhere else. And I am glad to have it. The rest of the week I am addicted to all those devices by which the average American is led to believe that a thing is important only if it is recent; that the biggest news is, *ipso facto*, the latest news. I read several daily papers; I listen to the news flashes on the radio and television, and every week buy three news magazines.

Then, on Sunday, I go to church. We sing the doxology, "Praise God From Whom All Blessings Flow." Some form of doxology has been sung by men and women at worship for at least 21 centuries. The hymns do not go back that far. But they go back far enough to be out of the running for the radio's Song Hits of the Week. I sang them on Sunday mornings when I was a boy. My father and mother sang them, and their parents before them. I like them for more than their age, but I do like them for that.

The minister reads the Old Testament lesson. That goes back farther than either the hymns or the doxology. It may go back 30 centuries—a thousand years before Christ. He reads the New Testament lesson, preferably in the King James Version. There is nothing new enough in what he reads to make the headlines. I heard the same passages in my youth. Men and women not very different from those in our church have heard them, generation before generation into the past. My children and their children will hear them generations into the future. They are more to me than a bridge to the past or the future. But they are that.

And before the preacher begins his sermon, I find that I have become consciously aware of something which, the rest of the week, is no more than a hunch. I realize that people like myself, with problems like mine, have been here a long time; that yesterday's newspapers did not say the first word and tomorrow's newspapers will not say the last word on anything. I know that tomorrow is another day. But I can say to myself: "Why so hurried, my little man?"

That is what I mean by perspective. I get that—a few minutes of it, at least—when I go to church. And that is more of it than I get anywhere else I go.

For another thing, I go to church because I like to be in a place, once in a while, where men take their hats off. I know all the places where, customarily, men's hats come off. What I mean is something more than custom. I suppose that "reverence" is the word for it. It may be just another survival from my youth, but I still find in my surroundings an atmosphere and in myself a sense of reverence when I go to church. I am glad that I do.

I think it is important to have something to revere—a banner, or a cause, or a person that is bigger than we are and better than we are when we are at our best; some place where, now and again, we can climb down from our high horses, and are in proportion. Bumptiousness is no virtue, despite its prevalence among intelligent people.

I have reservations, of course, when I go to church. I cannot, for example, go down the line word for word with the Apostles' Creed. For that matter, I do not take the church itself in my stride, as I once did. I have seen the ecclesiastical wheels go round, and I know that they are very much like any other wheels. Nevertheless, when I go to church I meet up with a great deal that I can still revere—more, in fact, than I meet up with anywhere else.

A few of my friends are intellectuals— ultra-ultras. They say that in an intelligent man's universe "there is no room for God." I never argue with them. But when I ask them what their "intelligent man's universe" does have room for, I stand in awe before the things that they admit nobody knows. On the next Sunday morning, therefore, I go to church. I go reverently, because I believe in God. But if I did not believe in Him, I would go anyway—out of reverence for the size of the mystery with which the little we know is surrounded.

Then, too, I go to church because the big idea back of what goes on there is to encourage whatever, in me, is good. My preacher does not go in very much for politics and economics. He just keeps hammering away on right and wrong. Sometimes I think he hammers away at me. But he is almost always right, and I take it.

It is very much like having an annual physical overhauling or seeing your dentist twice a year. Except that in the area where the church operates, I think most of us need to be overhauled oftener than that. I go to church because, after having sized things up all week by more or less selfish standards, I am ready for an hour in which they are sized up by moral standards. I can generally tell what I want to do without calling in any outside help. When it comes to deciding what is *right* to do, I can afford to have some counsel and advice.

The things that I get from my church are not offered anywhere else. And I have been going long enough to be sure, in my own mind, that I get along better with those things than without them.

* * *

I think we can see in Stanley High's article a

very honest and (on the surface at least) attractive statement of the reasons for going to church as presented by an average intelligent churchgoer. In most cases, if a person is asked, "Why do you go to church?" he gives the kind of answers that he thinks the pastor wants. In the case of High, he has been very honest and has stated his reasons without regard for what a pastor would like him to say. What reasons for churchgoing does High give? He lists five reasons: (1) He likes the preacher; (2) He finds it convenient; (3) Habit impels him; (4) He "gets something out of it," specifically, (a) historical perspective, (b) reverence for "a person that is bigger than we are," and (c) morality; (5) He "gets along better" as a result of churchgoing.

If we look closely at these reasons, we find that every one of them is *self-centered, not God-centered*. It may be of interest to you to know that there are no less than 112 instances of "I, my, mine, myself, me" in this article—which amounts to 4 first-person pronouns for every 3 lines of the article. The contrast with our Lord's words could hardly be greater:

> If any man will come after me, let him deny himself, and take up his cross, and follow me. For whosoever will save his life shall lose it: and whosoever will lose his life for my sake shall find it. For what is a man profited, if he shall gain the whole world and lose his own soul? (Matt. 16:24-26).

Notice also that in all the five reasons High

gives for churchgoing he mentions nothing that can't be gained outside the church: you can hear a good and inspiring speaker at any service club or political rally; convenience and habit can refer to moviegoing or TV watching as well as to church attendance; historical perspective can come by way of history courses (I ought to know!) or visits to museums and public libraries; reverence to something bigger than ourselves is available every time one sings "God save the Queen"; morality is inculcated in the Boy Scouts, the lodges, and in numerous other social organizations.

Consider further not just what High *includes*, but what he *omits*. He leaves out all reference to Christ; nowhere does he even mention the central message of the gospel, that "God was in Christ reconciling the world unto himself" (II Cor. 5:19). He totally omits the basic statement of the church's purpose, the Great Commission, "Go ye and teach all nations, baptizing them in the name of the Father, and of the Son, and of the Holy Ghost: teaching them to observe all things whatsoever I have commanded you" (Matt. 28:19-20). High's conception of God is so vague that he can say that he would go to church even if he didn't believe in God, "out of reverence for the size of the mystery with which the little we know is surrounded." He says he "cannot go down the line word for word with the Apostles' Creed": but what simpler or more basic statement of the essence of the Christian faith is there? If a person has trouble with this summary of central Christian doctrine, then I think we can question the whole conception of the church the man has.

There is certainly nothing the matter with reverence; and there is nothing the matter with morality. I love my mother as you love yours, and, like you, I try to avoid pushing old ladies under street cars! I am as much in favor of morality as the next man, and like most people I am "against sin." There is nothing the matter with hearing a good preacher, and there is nothing reprehensible about convenience or habit. But the question is, *What has all this to do with the essential nature of the church as revealed by and centered on Jesus Christ?*

I think that High's article well represents a groping toward the church. It is the honest preliminary statement of a person who comes to a pastor and says, "I think I'd like to become a church member; and these are some of the thoughts I have in mind." But I wonder seriously if this kind of an affirmation is appropriate for a person *within* the church—a person who has encountered the church as it is described in the New Testament. Now we have not yet analyzed what the church is in the New Testament, but in the next chapter we shall direct our attention to this problem. We are going to try to find out what the Bible has to say about the church, and to examine the contrasts between High's presentation and the presentation in the New Testament.

* * *

Many of you would say at this point: "All right, so Mr. High has a few misconceptions and leaves out a few things. The important thing is that he is going to church, and this is more important than anything else. He is bound to be a better man for it than he would be if he didn't go to church. His ideas aren't going to hurt anybody. The significant thing is that he is willing to go to a church and he certainly deserves more credit than the man who stays out on a golf course on Sunday morning." We have the idea that the church can do a person good only—that the church is an institution that can't hurt anybody. As I've heard people say very often, "It's better to go to church than not to go; it can't hurt you." Well, my friends, IT CAN HURT YOU, and that's one of the fundamental themes of this book.

In John 3:18 we read that anyone who does not receive from God the new birth from above through heart belief in Christ "is condemned already, because he hath not believed in the name of the only begotten Son of God"; and the risen Christ tells us that He will spue the lukewarm out of His mouth (Rev. 3:16). The church is no place for religious fellow-travellers. A man had better go to church for the right reasons—God-centered, not self-centered reasons—or not at all. The church can be a place of accelerated salvation; but it can also be a place of accelerated damnation. Which will it be for us?

CHAPTER TWO

The Biblical Conception
of Churchgoing

In the preceding chapter we considered the conception of churchgoing presented by Mr. Stanley High. As I mentioned, in my judgment his article is a very valuable one to analyze because it provides a transparent account by a layman of the reasons why he goes to church. I think that if we are really honest with ourselves many of us will have to say that our conception of churchgoing is not a great deal different from Mr. High's. There are many of us who look at churchgoing largely from the standpoints of convenience, morality, and perspective in the sense in which Mr. High uses these terms. A number of us, asked off-the-cuff by our friends what we get out of church, would probably answer in much the same way as Mr. High does.

We noticed that Mr. High's presentation lacks something; specifically, it lacks a foundation in Christ. Christ's name doesn't appear in Mr. High's article, and in his opinion the doctrines of the Apostles' Creed by no means represent the central elements in churchgoing. We are going to compare and contrast Mr. High's approach with the biblical conception of the church.

We are going to spend a great deal of time with the Scriptures (and let me say that in this respect at least I am a "ranting and raving fundamentalist"). I believe that the Bible is completely, entirely, and verbally the Word of God. I refuse to stand above and criticize it; I insist, rather, on standing below it and letting it criticize me. Now this may cause difficulties for some today, but I want to be perfectly honest with you: as far as I am concerned the conception of the church which is proper for a Christian is the conception of the church presented in the Bible. For me there is no other standard, and I see no possibility of arriving at any satisfactory answer to the problem of the nature of the church unless God has revealed it to us in Scripture.

First of all we shall see what the Bible says concerning the basic character of the church; and secondly we shall consider scriptural teaching as to the dangers of misunderstanding the nature of the church. The best starting point for learning about the New Testament idea of church is the word "church." Here is a golden opportunity to learn one Greek word—and *everybody* ought to know at least one Greek word! The word for church in the New Testament is *ecclesia,* from which we get the English words "ecclesiastic" and "ecclesiastical." This Greek word means literally "that which has been called out." The clear implication is that the church has been called *out of* something and *by* somebody. It has been called *out of the world,* and it has been called *by* God. Here we have the first two characteristics of the church: radical separation, and radical God-centeredness.

(1) *The church is a SEPARATED BODY.* Consider the following two biblical passages:

What fellowship has light with darkness? What accord has Christ with Belial? Or what has a believer in common with an unbeliever? What agreement has the temple of God with idols? For we are the temple of the living God; as God said, "I will live in them and move among them, and I will be their God, and they shall be my people. Therefore come out from them, and be separate from them, says the Lord, and touch nothing unclean; then I will welcome you, and I will be a father to you, and you shall be my sons and daughters, says the Lord Almighty."

After this I saw another angel coming down from heaven, having great authority; and the earth was made bright with his splendor, and he called out with a mighty voice, "Fallen, fallen is Babylon the great! It has become a dwelling place of demons, a haunt of every foul spirit, a haunt of every foul and hateful bird; for all nations have drunk the wine of her impure passion, and the kings of the earth have committed fornication with her, and the merchants of the earth have grown rich with the wealth of her wantonnesss." Then I heard another voice from heaven saying, "Come out of her, my people, lest you take part in her sins, lest you share in her plagues."

The first of these passages (II Cor. 6:14-18) refers in part to the sin of Christians marrying non-Christians, but it also has reference to the separation from the world which is mandatory for the church. The second passage (Rev. 18:1-4) strongly emphasizes that God's church must radically sever itself from a corrupt and unbelieving culture. In the early church, we know that Christians were so aware of the need for separation that they divided the service into two parts, the "mass of the catechumens" (like today's common service prior to Communion) and the "mass of the faithful" (like the Communion service itself), and they did not even allow the catechumens to attend the second part of the service!

What about us today? Mr. High says: "I go to church for the same reason that I go to the theater," and "it is very much like having an annual physical checkup or seeing your dentist." He regards the church as one organization among many human organizations. The New Testament, however, absolutely forbids this approach; the church is *not* like anything else. It is unique; it is separate. But, like Mr. High, we have so blurred the distinction between the church and the world that we make church membership ridiculously easy. Hardly any systematic instruction is necessary, and many join our churches without ever having given their lives to the Lord of the church,

Jesus Christ. The result? Weak or dead churches, filled with people who have more in common with the world than with the One who came into the world to seek and to save that which was lost.

(2) *The church is a separated body because it has been separated by God unto Himself; thus it CENTERS ON GOD, not on man.* Listen to Paul, writing under divine inspiration to the church at Ephesus (Eph. 1:20-23):

> He (God) raised him (Christ) from the dead, and made him sit at his right hand in the heavenly places, far above all rule and authority and power and dominion, and above every name that is named, not only in this age but also in that which is to come; and he has put all things under his feet and has made him the head over all things for the church, which is his body, the fullness of him who fills all in all.

This is a direct assertion that Christ is the center and foundation of the church. Contrast our attitude today: The church is *our* church—it centers on us, our needs, our social activities, our fellowship. We object when the pastor tells us we are wrong; after all, isn't he *our* pastor? didn't *we* choose him? Consider Mr. High again. He says he goes to church because "he gets something out of it." I suggest that the conception of the church as presented in Mr. High's article is not a God-centered conception of the church, not a Christ-centered conception of the church, but a thoroughly *man-centered* conception of the church. Mr. High's question is: What can the church do for me? God's question is: Do you acknowledge Christ's headship in the church? Thus the Bible presents a view of the church which is diametrically opposed to Mr. High's. It presents a church which is created not by human beings, but by God—by the God who separates human beings out of the world unto himself.

Now we move on to a third characteristic of the church as set forth in the Bible. We've discussed the radical God-centeredness of the church. Now we shall look at the constituency of the church. The church is (3) *a God-separated body of SAINTS.* The New Testament refers to church members as saints. The Greek word translated "saints" in the New Testament means "holy"—in the sense of separated. And the very same word is used in the expression "Holy Spirit"! Isn't it remarkable that the biblical writers employ the same word for the people who are in the church as for the Third Person of the Trinity! Why, it seems almost blasphemous; the least they could have done was to have used some other word! On the surface this looks like a kind of confusion between what God is and what we are, but if we think this way we misunderstand what the New Testament means by saint or holy person. A saint in the Bible is not a person who goes around telling children not to pick the wings off flies. Nor is the biblical saint a person going around in a long robe with a pious look on his face, or a person who sits in the desert and meditates. In the New Testament a saint is a person who has been *declared* holy by God—and not because of anything he has done, but because of something wonderful God has done for him.

How does a person enter this classification of saint? Consider I Cor. 1:1-2. This is the beginning of one of Paul's letters to the church at Corinth, and its salutation is typical of all of Paul's letters. He begins his letters in very much the same way no matter which church he writes to.

> Paul, called by the will of God to be an apostle of Christ Jesus, and our brother Sosthenes, to the church of God which is at Corinth, to those sanctified in Christ Jesus, called to be saints together with all those who in every place call on the name of our Lord Jesus Christ.

Note the parallel: Paul says that he was called by God to be an apostle, and the church members at Corinth have been called to be saints. In the New Testament Paul places a great deal of emphasis on the fact that he didn't make himself an apostle. He didn't become an apostle by making a great effort to become an apostle. He became an apostle because God made him one. And here he sets down a parallel between being called to be an apostle and being called to be a saint.

To become a saint, that is, to become one that is declared holy, one needs to be called by God. Now this begs the question. How is one called by God? One is called by God *through the preach-*

ing of the gospel. It is through the preaching of the gospel that a person hears God's call. If he responds to this call, if he receives the Christ who is presented, then he is declared holy by God. He can then be called a "saint," and he becomes a legitimate member of the New Testament church.

I think it worthwhile that we look at some examples of the way the apostles preached. We want to be very sure that what we consider the gospel is in fact what the apostles preached as the gospel. It seems to me that this is exceptionally important today because there are so many ideas prevalent as to what the gospel is. The apostles spent a good deal of time with our Lord, and if anybody knew what the gospel should be, it was the apostles themselves.

There is an interesting book that came out some years ago by C. H. Dodd, entitled *The Apostolic Preaching and Its Developments* (1936). In this book, Dodd goes through the sermons in the Book of Acts to see just how the apostles preached—to see what their message consisted of. We ourselves can take several examples from Acts and see just what kind of an apostolic gospel was presented to people in the first century. After all, it might just be that this is the kind of gospel *we* should be presenting in the church today as the basis of our own church membership! First, consider Peter's sermon at the beginning of the Book of Acts (Acts 2:36-42). This is the first sermon preached in the New Testament church. We're not going to exam-

ine all of it, just the ending of it, and the effect
it had on those present.

> Let all the house of Israel therefore know
> assuredly that God has made him both Lord
> and Christ, this Jesus whom you crucified.
> Now when they heard this they were cut
> to the heart, and said to Peter and the rest of
> the apostles, "Brethren, what shall, we
> do?" And Peter said to them, "Repent,
> and be baptized every one of you in the name
> of Jesus Christ for the forgiveness of your
> sins; and you shall receive the gift of the
> Holy Spirit. For the promise is to you and to
> your children and to all that are far off, every
> one whom the Lord our God calls to him."
> And he testified with many other words and
> exhorted them, saying, "Save yourselves
> from this crooked generation." So those who
> received his word were baptized, and there
> were added that day about three thousand
> souls. And they devoted themselves to the
> apostles' teaching and fellowship, to the
> breaking of bread and the prayers.

Note the emphases: the people have been *called,*
and if they respond they will receive the gift of the
Holy Spirit, i.e., they will become holy people—
saints. What decision must they make? A decision for the crucified Jesus, for "God has made
him both Lord and Christ." The man whom these
people had crucified was their Lord. And as Peter
preached, the people were cut to the heart; they
saw that they were guilty before God for having
mistreated Jesus—that they had mistreated the
revelation God had provided in Jesus. And when

they recognized this they said, "What can we do to be saved?" And the straight answer was: receive Him; receive this Christ. *These, then, are the two steps involved in the gospel: recognizing one's need, and recognizing that Christ is the answer to that need.*

One of the great theologians of our time, Paul Tillich, stressed that every man has a god, for every man has an ultimate commitment. It may be to his bowling league, it may be to his family, it may be to his job; it can be to any of a vast number of things. But every man has a god; every man has something that is more important to him than anything else. What Peter did in his sermon was to show that the *true* God is the one who came in the person of Jesus Christ, that everybody is guilty before this true God, and that commitment must be to *Him*—and not to anyone or anything else. There can't be any compromise.

Now let's look at the preaching of Philip, another apostle. This is a personal witnessing encounter recorded in Acts 8:26-39.

> But an angel of the Lord said to Philip, "Rise and go toward the south to the road that goes down from Jerusalem to Gaza." This is a desert road. And he rose and went. And behold, an Ethiopian, a eunuch, a minister of Candace the queen of the Ethiopians, in charge of all her treasure, had come to Jerusalem to worship and was returning; seated in his chariot, he was reading the prophet Isaiah. And the Spirit said to Philip,

"Go up and join this chariot." So Philip ran to him, and heard him reading Isaiah the prophet, and asked, "Do you understand what you are reading?" And he said, "How can I, unless some one guides me?" And he invited Philip to come up and sit with him.

Now the passage of the scripture which he was reading was this:

"As a sheep led to the slaughter
or a lamb before its shearer is dumb,
so he opens not his mouth.
In his humiliation justice was denied him.
Who can describe his generation?
For his life is taken up from the earth."

And the eunuch said to Philip, "About whom, pray, does the prophet say this, about himself or about some one else?" Then Philip opened his mouth, and beginning with this scripture he told him the good news of Jesus. And as they went along the road they came to some water, and the eunuch said, "See, here is water! What is to prevent my being baptized?" And he commanded the chariot to stop, and they both went down into the water, Philip and the eunuch, and he baptized him. And when they came up out of the water, the Spirit of the Lord caught up Philip; and the eunuch saw him no more, and went on his way rejoicing.

The eunuch was trying to understand the Scriptures. He read about somebody suffering, and Philip told him that the person who was suffering was Jesus—that the suffering of Jesus fulfilled the Old Testament. And when the eunuch saw that fulfillment both of the Old Testament and of one's personal life comes in the good news of Jesus, he said, "What hinders me from being baptized?" Forthwith baptism took place just as it did after Peter's preaching; the man became a Christian; and the glorious results were due to the work of the Holy Spirit.

Consider one other example of the preaching that the apostles carried on. In this case Paul is the preacher, and the incident is the famous one of the Philippian jailer. We are going to look at a little bit of it (Acts 16:27-34). You remember that Paul and his companions had been jailed, and as a result of divine activity Paul was released.

> When the jailer woke and saw that the prison doors were open, he drew his sword and was about to kill himself, supposing that the prisoners had escaped. But Paul cried with a loud voice, "Do not harm yourself, for we are all here." And he called for lights and rushed in, and trembling with fear he fell down before Paul and Silas, and brought them out and said, "Men, what must I do to be saved?" And they said, "Believe in the Lord Jesus, and you will be saved, you and your household." And they spoke the word of the Lord to him and to all that were in his house. And he took them the same hour of the night, and washed their wounds, and he was baptized at once, with all his family. Then he brought them up into his house, and set food before them; and he rejoiced with all his household that he had believed in God.

Here again, the same pattern: a recognition of

need ("What must I do to be saved?"), and the apostolic presentation of Jesus as the answer to the need. This is especially interesting in the Greek, by the way, because the word "believe" here is in a special form which says in effect, "Do it now, don't wait!" This is the actual meaning of the form, that one must act immediately; decision for Christ is not something you can put off. Do it now; there may not be another opportunity. And the Greek says "believe *into*"—"believe *into* the Lord Jesus." Don't just have an intellectual knowledge of Him, but rely upon Him. Enter into Him by faith. When the King James Bible says "believe *on*," it is trying to get across that meaning of the Greek.

I heard a good illustration of the meaning of this "on" or "into," and I will pass it along to you. The story is told of a Christian businessman who was attending a convention in a city, and while he was staying at the convention hotel he tried to present the gospel to the hotel elevator boy. The elevator boy said, "I can understand what it means to believe *in* Jesus, to believe something about Jesus—I'm a church member myself—but what's this 'believing on' business?" The convention continued for a day or so, and finally the businessman had to leave. He rang for the elevator, and the elevator came up to his floor, stopped, and the door opened. The businessman just stood outside with his bags. The elevator boy said, "Did you ring?"; the businessman replied, "Yes." The boy said, "What floor do you want to go to?" The Christian said, "I want to go to the main floor," but still stood there. The elevator boy said, "Well, then, what's the matter?" The Christian replied, "Nothing's the matter. I believe that the elevator has the power to take me to the first floor." And still he stood there. In exasperation the elevator boy cried, "What's the matter with you? It won't do you any good to believe in the elevator unless you get ON it!" And the businessman said, "This is exactly what it means when the Bible says, 'Believe *on* the Lord Jesus and you shall be saved.'"

That is the idea of this "into," this "on." One must depend upon Christ, rely on Him, "get on board." It isn't sufficient just to have intellectual knowledge in order to be saved; belief must be both of the head and of the heart. This is the kind of message that is presented as the gospel in the preaching of the Book of Acts, and I think we ought to see that the whole center of attention is not on the person who is doing the believing, but on God in Christ who calls the person, and on whom the person must rely. Again and again the apostles stress what *God* does, not what the person himself does. This is one of the great emphases of Luther. He always said in effect: "Stop looking to yourself; look to the Cross. If you look upon yourself long enough you will become utterly wretched, and may never find the answer. Look rather to the Christ."

Now, I don't want to make Mr. High appear worse than he really is, but it is necessary to take another glance at his article. Look at the concluding paragraphs of his essay. Mr. High's climax comes in the matter of ethics—morality—DOING GOOD. High says, for example, "I go to church because the big idea back of what goes on there is to encourage whatever, in me, is good." Now, I may be wrong, but as far as I can tell, this is not what one finds in the apostolic preaching. In the apostolic preaching, the emphasis is not on bringing out any goodness in anybody. The emphasis in the apostolic preaching is on man seeing his need—on the fact that man hasn't got any good within him, and that he desperately needs to rely on Jesus Christ for everything.

This ties in with what we said before about God-centeredness versus man-centeredness. In the Bible you never find moralism and do-goodishness. Romans 12:9ff has ethical commands in it, but it follows directly on Paul's statement of the gospel. The first half of the Book of Romans consists of Paul's presentation of the gospel, and the last half consists of Paul's ethical advice *based and centered on what Christ has done.* All the way through the New Testament, you find exactly the same situation. Never is morality stressed as such. It is stressed only as a response to what God has already done for us in Jesus Christ.

Contrast also with the apostolic message Mr. High's emphasis on "liking the preacher." I am not so sure that the people who heard Peter's sermon liked it. The account says that they were cut to the heart and cried, "What shall we do?" It frightens me when a person comes to me after a sermon I have delivered and says, "I liked it." Now, what does he mean by this? Is he trying to tell me that he likes me and wants me to know that we are friends? I would like somebody to come up to me some day and say, "I was cut to the heart."

Consider Mr. High's emphasis on habit as a basis for churchgoing, and note the situation of the Ethiopian eunuch. All of his habits would have directed him somewhere else than the gospel of Christ. In his background there was nothing habitual to drive him to Christ. What drove the Ethiopian eunuch to Christ was Christ's own word as conveyed by Philip. This is very important, because conscience structured by habit can drive people in many, many directions—maybe towards the gospel, maybe away from the gospel. I know people whose habit it is to sleep in on Sunday morning, and it would violate their consciences if they got up and did anything else. Conscience, you see, is always conditioned by one's past. For example, if Junior sticks his little paw into the cookie jar and gets whacked a sufficient number of times, he will feel guilty about sticking his little paw in the cookie jar. On the other hand, if Junior's papa happens to be a shoplifter, and papa instructs Junior in the fine art of lifting items from the five-and-dime, Junior will feel conscience-stricken if he misses a good opportunity. Therefore one must be awfully careful on the matter of habit.

There is no emphasis at all in the Bible on habit in this sense, as far as I can determine. The emphasis is entirely upon God's Word breaking in on a man, regardless of what his habitual activity has been.

We have now discussed three characteristics of the church: the characteristic of separation, the characteristic of God-centeredness, and the characteristic of sainthood. The church is different from all other societies; it is created and sustained by God, not man; and its criterion of membership is sainthood. To become a true member of this God-centered, separated body, a man must become a saint, and he becomes a saint *not* because of anything in him, not because of anything he can do, but only by accepting in faith what God has already done for him through Christ's saving death on the Cross.

We have one final point with regard to the nature of the church, and this has to do with (4) *its purpose: The church has one single and central purpose according to the New Testament, and this purpose is to PREACH THE GOSPEL.* You can often get a pretty good idea of a man's basic concern from his last words. This isn't always the case, to be sure, for there have been famous people whose last words are of no more profundity than "May I have a glass of water." But in the case our Lord, since His last word was given before ascending into heaven, when He was fully aware of what He was doing, we can be quite sure that

He was saying something that He wanted emphasized above everything else in His church. Let's
take a look at Acts 1:6-8, where Jesus' last encounter with His disciples is described.

> When they therefore were come together,
> they asked of him, saying, Lord, wilt thou
> at this time restore again the kingdom to
> Israel? And he said unto them, It is not for
> you to know the times or the seasons, which
> the Father hath put in his own power. But
> ye shall receive power, after that the Holy
> Ghost is come upon you: and ye shall be wit-
> nesses unto me both in Jerusalem, and in all
> Judaea, and in Samaria, and unto the utter-
> most part of the earth.

If you have ever outlined the Book of Acts, you
know that it follows the missionary pattern of
Jesus' words. The gospel moves out from Jerusa-
lem, to Judaea, to Samaria, and finally it reaches
the very center of the earth as it was known at
that time, Rome. When Paul arrives at Rome,
then, in a very real sense, the gospel has reached
the uttermost parts of the earth, because "all roads
lead to Rome"—and out of it. The gospel will
spread out along all the roads leading from Rome
to the rest of the world.

In this passage, Jesus presents the command
to witness—the same command you all know as the
Great Commission, given at the very end of the
Gospel of Matthew. I wonder if we do consider this
the real function of the church—the central function of the church. It doesn't appear anywhere in
Mr. High's article. There is no suggestion in Mr.

High's article that the church member ought to present anything to anybody else. I am sure that Mr. High would not object to inviting someone to a church supper, or the like, but even such a minimal witness is lacking in the article. Mr. High apparently thinks that one can deal with church membership without ever mentioning witness. Mr. High speaks vaguely about reverence to "the mystery" that is about us, but Jesus told His apostles to go out and preach a gospel to every creature, and this gospel has specific content: the fact that Jesus himself is God, that He came to earth to die for the sins of the world, that He was raised again. Paul specifies the gospel in a very clean-cut manner in I Cor. 15:1-4.

> Now I would remind you, brethren, in what terms I preached to you the gospel, which you received, in which you stand, by which you are saved, if you hold it fast— unless you believed in vain. For I delivered to you as of first importance what I also received, that Christ died for our sins in accordance with the scriptures, that he was buried, that he was raised on the third day in accordance with the scriptures.

The Christian religion is not a vague matter of reverence or mystery. If you want reverence or mystery, you can get this anywhere. This is not the reason the church is in existence. The church is in existence to PREACH THE GOSPEL. The apostles did not sit around having mystic experiences. They went out and preached the gospel until they couldn't preach it anymore—until they were physically stopped by death from doing this. And, interestingly enough, we are Christians today because they did preach the gospel. I seriously question whether we would be Christians today if they had spent their time talking about reverence, about liking preachers, about convenience, about moral values, about historical perspective.

It is one of the great tragedies of modern history that so few missionaries went to China when they had the chance. During the nineteenth century it was possible for any number of missionaries to go from our churches to China, and hardly anybody went. A very small impact was made on China for the gospel; and today we are reaping the judgment of God on ourselves because of our indifference. We are frightened silly of China today, and we have every right to be. The Chinese situation is more serious than even the Russian situation because the Chinese have not had the benefit of Western values with regard to the worth of the individual. The Chinese communists are quite willing to sacrifice themselves (or others) for their cause, and they don't think twice about the individual. If they do decide to move, you and I are going to be in a very uncomfortable position. I suggest that if we had carried out Christ's Commission to preach the gospel to every creature, in the way the Scripture sets it forth for us, we would not have this problem today. A man who is a Christian, who believes in God, who believes that Jesus died on the Cross for his sins, cannot accept atheistic, materialistic Marxism. But the Chinese, who were still in the vague area of Confucian morality when communism arrived, accepted Marxism without much difficulty, for we had not preached the gospel to them.

Now you sit back and say, "How fortunate I am that I wasn't born in the nineteenth century; that certainly isn't my problem." But right now the same situation is duplicating itself in Africa. Today, Christians can get into Africa and preach the gospel. Perhaps this will not be the case twenty years from now, with rising tides of nationalism. What are you doing about this? You know that there is a tremendous need for lay missionaries, not just for people who have had seminary training, but for people who will carry out their own jobs on the foreign mission field. This is a desperate need. Many people volunteer for the Peace Corps, but how many of us seriously consider giving up our comforts and our convenience here at home to do what God tells us to do—to fulfill the central aim of His church by proclaiming His gospel to the ends of the earth?

* * *

Having analyzed the New Testament concept of the church, and having contrasted it with the popular view as presented by Stanley High, we must ask the inevitable question: What is the danger in holding a wrong conception of the church? At the outset at least some of us would have said, "Well, you can't expect everything of people; the important thing is not *why* people go to church, but *whether* they go." In the subways of New York, there frequently appears a sign which says, "Go to church this Sunday—you'll feel better for it." I am not saying that you won't feel better, but it may be that you ought not to feel better. What we want to see is what the New Testament has to say about the dangers of misunderstanding the nature of the church.

Let's take a look at the Old Testament background for a moment. The person who says, "Isn't it marvellous that people go to church," feels that there is nothing negative that can happen to people as a result of their churchgoing. Such a person really ought also to say, "How wonderful it must have been for the Israelites; how jolly to have been an Israelite! Ah, to have been one of the Chosen People, wandering about in the desert with God directly guiding." But consider I Cor. 10:5-12, where Paul is talking about the Israelites who were in the wilderness:

> Nevertheless with most of them God was not pleased; for they were overthrown in the wilderness. Now these things are warnings for us, not to desire evil as they did. Do not be idolaters as some of them were; as it is written, "The people sat down to eat and drink and rose up to dance." We must not indulge in immorality as some of them did, and twenty-three thousand fell in a single day. We must not put the Lord to the test, as some of them did and were destroyed by ser-

pents; nor grumble, as some of them did and were destroyed by the Destroyer. Now these things happened to them as a warning, but they were written down for our instruction, upon whom the end of the ages has come. Therefore let any one who thinks that he stands take heed lest he fall.

This sobering account does not have to do with a misconception of the church as such, but it does indicate that it was *dangerous* to be an Israelite. When the people had been out in the desert for a while with their God, they said, "Would that we had stayed in Egypt." Why? *Because when they went out under God's command they put themselves in a position where God expected more of them than He would have otherwise.* This is why defection in the wilderness was immediately followed by judgment—by horrible judgment. A vast number "were destroyed by the Destroyer." And let us not forget that "these things were written down for our instruction." In Rom. 2:9-10, we read, furthermore:

There will be tribulation and distress for every human being who does evil, the Jew first and also the Greek; but glory and honor and peace for every one who does good, the Jew first and also the Greek.

Judgment, according to Paul, comes first upon the Jew, and blessing comes first upon the Jew. Why? Because God chose the Jew. Note that there is no double standard: it isn't that the Chosen People are to receive the blessings first and the other people get condemnation first. The Chosen receive *both* blessings *and* condemnation first, because they have been called by God. Being called by God, then, is a dangerous proposition.

Now we shall look at an event in the early church which should give us pause. I refer to the story of Ananias and Sapphira in Acts 5:1-11:

> But a man named Ananias with his wife Sapphira sold a piece of property, and with his wife's knowledge he kept back some of the proceeds, and brought only a part and laid it at the apostles' feet. But Peter said, "Ananias, why has Satan filled your heart to lie to the Holy Spirit and to keep back part of the proceeds of the land? While it remained unsold, did it not remain your own? And after it was sold, was it not at your disposal? How is it that you have contrived this deed in your heart? You have not lied to men but to God." When Ananias heard these words, he fell down and died. And great fear came upon all who heard of it. The young men arose and wrapped him up and carried him out and buried him.

> After an interval of about three hours his wife came in, not knowing what had happened. And Peter said to her, "Tell me whether you sold the land for so much." And she said, "Yes, for so much." But Peter said to her, "How is it that you have agreed together to tempt the Spirit of the Lord? Hark, the feet of those that have buried your husband are at the door, and they will carry you out." Immediately she fell down at his feet and died. When the young men came in they found her dead, and they carried her out and buried her beside her husband. And great fear

came upon the whole church, and upon all
who heard of these things.

I suggest that the greatest mistake Ananias and
Sapphira ever made was to join the church. This
was a serious tactical error on their part. If they
wanted to live hypocritically as members of a man-
centered social organization, then they never in the
world should have joined the church, because the
result for them was catastrophic: they lost their
lives. This certainly would not have happened to
them if they hadn't misunderstood the nature of
God's church.

In I Cor. 11:27-30, Paul has this to say to those
who misunderstand the Lord's Supper:

> Whoever, therefore, eats the bread or
> drinks the cup of the Lord in an unworthy
> manner will be guilty of profaning the body
> and blood of the Lord. Let a man examine
> himself, and so eat of the bread and drink of
> the cup. For any one who eats and drinks
> without discerning the body eats and drinks
> judgment upon himself. That is why many of
> you are weak and ill, and some have died.

Here Paul says specifically that physical illness
and even physical death have resulted from misunderstanding the purpose of the central rite of the
Christian church. You may think that this is super-
stition, that this is silly, that death and illness could
not possibly result from the taking of the Lord's
Supper, but this is exactly what the apostle asserts
—and under divine inspiration.

In Hebrews 6:4-9, the writer makes an even
stronger statement:

For it is impossible to restore again to repentance those who have once been enlightened, who have tasted the heavenly gift, and have become partakers of the Holy Spirit, and have tasted the goodness of the word of God and the powers of the age to come, if they then commit apostasy, since they crucify the Son of God on their own account and hold him up to contempt. For land which has drunk the rain that often falls upon it, and brings forth vegetation useful to those for whose sake it is cultivated, receives a blessing from God. But if it bears thorns and thistles, it is worthless and near to being cursed; its end is to be burned. Though we speak thus, yet in your case, beloved, we feel sure of better things that belong to salvation.

Here we are told that the person who has once tasted "the heavenly gift," that is, the gospel, cannot, if he falls away, be restored. This means that hearing the gospel can put a person in an extremely dangerous situation.

In Matt. 12:31 and Mark 3:29 our Lord speaks of the so-called "unpardonable sin"—the sin against the Holy Ghost. It is the refusal to receive God's grace as God's grace. Some people say that this is refusing to go to church. In some lives I think it is, but in many other lives it is *willingness to go to church but refusal to look at the church as Christ wants us to look at it*—refusal to regard the church as the place where men stand at the foot of the Cross and are saved solely by God's grace.

The passages just discussed illustrate one of the most central principles in the entire Scripture, but a principle that is not very often emphasized, namely, that GOD NEVER COMES IN NEUTRALITY; HE ALWAYS COMES EITHER IN JUDGMENT OR IN GRACE. If He doesn't come in grace, then He comes in judgment. If He is not received as He should be received, He comes in judgment. As someone has well put it: "The same sun that melts the ice, hardens the clay." This melting and hardening goes on in the church all the time. Hearts are melted, but other hearts are hardened. The more a man hears the gospel and disregards it, the harder his heart becomes, and the more difficult it is for him to understand what the gospel is really saying to him.

The conclusion is, then, that DAMNATION THROUGH THE CHURCH IS A LIVE POSSIBILITY, not just a clever phrase originating with this writer. We had better be very sure that we see the true nature of the church and do not try to make over the church in our image. If we do the latter, we take a terrible risk. We actually imperil our souls if we view the church as a man-centered organization indistinguishable from a social club; to be saved through the church we must see it as the one God-given agency on earth through which we can come to know Christ our Savior and proclaim His saving love to others.

In the next chapter we shall take a rapid tour through several epochs of church history, including our own period, and see what kind of misconceptions of the church people have had and continue to have. Mr. High provides us with no more than an introduction to the ways in which we human beings tend to pervert the church of the New Testament. Finally, after bringing into sharp focus our misunderstandings and distortions of the church, we shall endeavor in the last chapter to see what can be done about this situation. Our aim will be to discover how we can avoid damnation through the church, and how it is possible for us to be saved through that same God-given, grace-sustained community of worship and witness.

CHAPTER THREE

Damnable Epochs in Church History

Now we are going to deal with some problems in the understanding of the church through the centuries, and at the end of the chapter we shall focus our attention on our own church today. This chapter gives me a chance to play my chief role as historian, and this may well make some of you feel a bit edgy, since I am going to deal with the past. As one of my students once said to me, "I wouldn't mind history so much if it didn't deal with the past." Another student said to me, "Why do we always have to talk about people who are dead?" Unfortunately, there is no way of avoiding this if you deal with a historical topic! The value of examining history is that one can acquire a greater perspective on our situation at the present time. And the problems we are going to talk about in several periods of church history are problems that still remain with us today. First I am going to discuss with you four periods of church history in which the nature of the church was badly misunderstood by many religious people; then I am going to speak about four ecclesiastical misconceptions which, I believe, we today have added to the misunderstandings inherited from the past.

We begin with the church in Luther's day. It is not going to be necessary to say very much about the church in Luther's time because you probably know a great deal about it already. You know that Luther was deeply disturbed about the religious situation of the early sixteenth century. He felt that the church of his day was, in many respects, causing more harm than good because it misunderstood the basic character of the gospel. And Luther pulled no punches; he stated exactly what the problem was; he let the chips fall where they might. Luther's main objection to the church of his time was not, however, what some of us think it was. Some of us wrongly think that Luther was mainly objecting to a lack of freedom of thought in the church. I have heard a number of Reformation Day sermons in which the preacher says: "Back in the Dark Ages people were compelled to believe things—ridiculous and irrational things. Then came the Reformation and men's minds were made free. With the Reformation it became possible for a man to believe anything he wanted to. Now our conscience can be our sole guide in matters of belief." Now, if you think that this was the case, then you simply don't understand what the Reformation was all about. There was probably no more "bigoted" a person who ever lived than Martin Luther. He was a person who was so bigoted that he said on the most crucial occasion of his life—at the Imperial Diet at Worms—"My conscience is captive to the Word of God." Luther did not permit his conscience to run free. He subjected his conscience to the Word of God, that is, to the living Christ and to the presentation of the living Christ given to us in the Holy Scriptures. The purpose of the Reformation was not to bring about "freedom of thought." Luther would have been horrified at the degree to which many churches today allow themselves to modify or ignore biblical doctrine.

Luther's actual objection to the church of his day was that it had become an end in itself, and no longer a means to an end. Luther's real objection was that the church had become SACRAMENTALISTIC, that is to say, people went to church feeling that if they took part in the prescribed sacramental rituals, in some automatic fashion their problem of God-relationship would be taken care of for them. They regarded the sacramental rites *ex opere operato,* as works having power already inherent in them—as virtually automatic means of salvation. They made the terrible mistake of considering the church a magical agency that dissolves a person's spiritual problems. Listen to what Luther had to say on this subject:

> Neither Sacrament nor priest, but faith in the Word of Christ, mediated through the priest and his office, justifies you. What concern of yours would it be if the Lord spoke through an ass as long as you hear His Word,

in which you may hope and believe? (*WA* 1, 595)

This is typical Luther, strong language and all! Luther—unlike many preachers—did not care if his words shocked people; his concern was to make clear exactly what the real issues were. Luther says in effect: "It really does not make any difference if the pastor is an ass. The important thing is that the Word of God is preached. Nobody is saved through a pastor, whether he is an ass or not. A man is saved by the Word of God." In another place Luther said this:

> Accursed into the abyss of hell be all obedience that is rendered to government, father, and mother, yea, and the church, too, at the cost of being disobedient to God! If God commanded and required me to do something, how could He possibly be expected to look on and tolerate my rationalizing, my disobedience, by saying: Lord, the Christian Church told me to do this? None of that! He would reply, the Christian Church means nothing in this case; but simply spurn with your feet whatever all the angels, saints, and all the world may command you to do, and frankly say: I recognize neither the father, the mother, the relative, the government, nor the Christian Church that wants to prevent me from listening to God's Word. (*WA* 28, 24)

Luther did not, of course, eliminate the use of sacraments in the church. He didn't exclude Means of Grace, properly understood. But he did make clear that the church and its Means of Grace are not magical, and that people who regard the church as an automatic way to heaven are in real danger of hell. The church of Luther's day had a ghastly tendency to look at its sacraments as providing an irrevocable insurance policy. Incidentally, I get the impression when listening to some Christians today that they think of Confirmation in this fashion—as a kind of insurance policy. Certainly in Luther's day there were many people who felt that the sacramental system of the church was a great fire insurance policy which would preserve them from damnation; yet, as Luther says, to take this view is *really* to play with fire, for it substitutes the church for the Lord of the church, Jesus Christ.

Just so that we don't get the idea that Luther is the last word on this (or any!) issue, I shall quote a passage on the same subject from Holy Writ (Amos 5:21-27):

I hate, I despise your feast days, and I will not smell in your solemn assemblies. Though ye offer me burnt offerings and your meat offerings, I will not accept them: neither will I regard the peace offerings of your fat beasts. Take thou away from me the noise of thy songs; for I will not hear the melody of thy viols. But let judgment run down as waters, and righteousness as a mighty stream. Have ye offered unto me sacrifices and offerings in the wilderness forty years, O house of Israel? But ye have borne the tabernacle of your Moloch and Chiun your images, the star of your god, which ye made to yourselves. Therefore will

I cause you to go into captivity.

Here the prophet Amos, by the inspiration of the Lord, says to the people of Israel—and to all "religious" people: "Your sacrifices and your burnt offerings mean absolutely nothing as long as idolatry exists in your midst." For many people in Luther's day, the church was the great sacramental idol.

Now we move on to a later period in church history, the time of Napoleon. Napoleon himself, during his exile on St. Helena, had a conversation with a certain Count Montholon; in the course of their discussion Napoleon commented on his own religious views. This is what Napoleon supposedly said:

> Alexander, Caesar, Charlemagne, and I myself have founded great empires . . . upon force. Jesus alone founded His Empire upon love. . . . Jesus Christ was more than a man. . . . He asks for the human heart: He demands it unconditionally. . . . All who sincerely believe in Him experience that remarkable supernatural love towards Him. . . . Time, the great destroyer, is powerless to extinguish this sacred flame. . . . This it is which proves to me quite convincingly the divinity of Jesus Christ!

This, I think, is a very revealing statement. The most revealing thing about it is that it came *after* Napoleon had arrived on St. Helena. Had Napoleon recognized these truths earlier in his career, his goal of conquest would certainly have been altered.

The church in Napoleon's day was in a very,

very bad state because it substituted RATIONAL-
ISM for the Word of God. During the time of the
French Revolution a religious viewpoint called
"Deism" came into the church. This view held that
only a God who could be understood rationally
should be accepted by the church; anything which
was irrational or unreasonable should be eliminated from religion. What this did in effect was to
make Reason into a god.

One of the most important figures during the
Napoleonic era was Thomas Paine (1737-1809).
Thomas Paine is a favorite of U.S. citizens because
he had a great deal to do with the Declaration of
Independence. Thomas Paine was a great patriot,
one must admit, but at the same time he was a
wretched theologian. He placed Reason above the
Scriptures—as we see from his book entitled, *The
Age of Reason*. The first part of this book consists
of his argument in behalf of Reason, and the second part consists entirely of an attempt to show
that the Bible is full of contradictions and errors,
a work that should not be relied on ethically,
morally, or in any other sense. At the very end
of his book Paine writes:

> It has been my wandering from the im-
> mutable laws of science, and right use of
> reason, and setting up an invented thing
> called revealed religion, that so many wild
> and blasphemous conceits have been formed
> of the Almighty. The Jews have made him
> the assassin of the human species to make
> room for the religion of the Jews. The Chris-
> tians have made him the murderer of him-

self and the founder of a new religion, to supersede and expel the Jewish religion. And to find pretense and admission for these things, they must have supposed his power or his wisdom imperfect, or his will changeable; and the changeableness of the will is imperfection of the judgment. The philosopher knows that the laws of the Creator have never changed with respect either to the principles of science, or the properties of matter.

During the so-called "Age of Reason," many people thought this way. At the time of the French Revolution, which eventually brought Napoleon to power, the Revolutionists decreed (Nov. 9, 1793) that God did not exist and that the worship of Reason was to be substituted instead. A veiled female was brought before the Convention, and Chaumette, taking her by the hand, said, "Mortals, cease to tremble before the powerless thunders of a God whom your fears have created. Henceforth, acknowledge no divinity but Reason. I offer you its noblest and purest image; if you must have idols, sacrifice only to such as this." The veil fell, and the woman proved to be Madame Maillard, of the Opéra. Mounted on a magnificent car, she was taken by the crowd to Notre Dame, to take the place of Deity. There, elevated on the altar, she received the adoration of all who were present.

This Notre Dame incident well illustrates Luther's contention that Reason can be "the devil's whore," that is Reason can corrupt the Christian faith at its very center if it is set against the Word of God. Luther admitted that he did not rationally understand all the great doctrines of the Faith, but he said that just like a peasant he would remove his cap before divinely revealed truths. This was Luther, a Doctor of Holy Scripture, a man who held the highest academic degree of his day, but a man who refused to set his reason against the Word of God. Luther also said that if God told him to go out in the field and eat an ear of corn because grace would come that way, he would do it no matter how foolish it seemed. By this he was trying to point out that in God's mercy and love He has told us many things—such as that we are to be baptized "for the remission of sins"—which to ordinary reason have no meaning at all, and yet which are profoundly meaningful because God himself stands behind them.

Remember the words of Holy Scripture? In Isaiah, God says (Isa. 55:8-9):

> My thoughts are not your thoughts, neither are your ways my ways, saith the Lord. For as the heavens are higher than the earth, so are my ways higher than your ways, and my thoughts than your thoughts.

And He assures us in Second Peter (II Pet. 1:21):

> Prophecy came not in old time by the will of man, but holy men of God spake as they were moved by the Holy Ghost.

But during Napoleon's day Reason was set up as an idol in the church, and Christ was put aside.

Now we come to nineteenth-century Denmark. Here we meet Søren Kierkegaard (1813-

1855), a Danish philosopher who was very, very disturbed with the church situation of his time. Kierkegaard looked about the city of Copenhagen, and everywhere he saw "Christians"—but they were Christians in quotation marks. He saw professed Christians who were completely secure and self-satisfied, for they "had" the Bible. Many of them carried the Bible in their pockets; they *had* the Word of God—it was theirs—and life went on peaceably, happily, in a well-adjusted fashion. Kierkegaard asked himself if this is really the religion which is set forth in the Bible. His answer was that such religion is an "impudent indecency"; listen to one of his milder statements (*Papirer,* Danis ed., XI, 1. A347):

A young girl of sixteen summers;—it is her confirmation day. Among the many tasteful and beautiful gifts she also receives the New Testament in a very pretty binding.

Now, that is what one may call Christianity! To tell the truth, no one expects— and probably rightly—that she, any more than anybody else, will read it, or at any rate not as originally intended. This book was given her as a potential consolation in life; here, should you need it, you will find consolation; of course it is assumed that she will never read it, any more than other young girls, but if she does, it will not be read as originally intended, or she would discover that right there in that book you find such terrors that, in comparison, other terrible things that occur in the world are almost a joke.

Yet that is supposed to be Christianity....

No, I would be tempted to make Christianity another proposition: Let us gather in every single copy of the New Testament, let us cart the whole collection out to an open place, or up a mountain top, and then, while all of us kneel down, let someone speak to God, saying: Take it back, this book; we humans, the way we are, should not get involved with such a book; it only makes us unhappy. Now, I suggest that, like those townspeople of yore, we ask Christ to take another road.

The problem in Kierkegaard's Danish church was DEAD ORTHODOXY. The Danes of his time didn't put Reason above the Bible. No sir! For them the Bible was such an authority that they never read it. It was on everybody's front table, and it was in everybody's pocket, but nobody read it; and for this reason they never encountered the God who spoke in thunder from Sinai, and, even more tragically, they never encountered the God who spoke words of eternal forgiveness from the Cross.

Now I pass on to the fourth "damnable epoch in church history": the church of Hitler's Germany, where POLITICISM prevailed. For many of you this is contemporary history, and it has a very close parallel to the situation in one part of the world at this very moment. In Hitler's day, politics and government were substituted for the Christian faith, and the church was turned into something which was anything but a divine institution. In Hit-

ler's Germany there was a movement sponsored
and promoted by the Nazi party to change the character of Christianity. The people who supported this
movement were known as the "Deutsche Christen"
—the "German Christians" or "German Christian
Faith Movement." Among other things, this movement eliminated the Old Testament because it had
so many references to the Jews. Then it eliminated
or altered portions of the New Testament—particularly those sections presenting Jesus in a Jewish
frame of reference, because the Nazi party was
against the Jews. Typical of the "German Christians" was Dr. Hans Kerrl, who was appointed by
Hitler to be Minister for Church Affairs. In 1937,
Kerrl delivered a speech in which he said:

> Positive Christianity *is* National Social-
> ism. . . . National Socialism is the doing of
> God's will. . . . God's will reveals itself in
> German Blood. . . . The main thing is deeds.
> Christianity is not dependent upon the Apos-
> tles' Creed. . . . True Christianity is repre-
> sented by the party, and the German Volk are
> now called by the party and especially the
> Fuehrer to a real Christianity. . . . The
> Church has not been able to generate the
> faith that moves mountains. But the Fuehrer
> has! The Fuehrer is the herald of a new reve-
> lation. (Quoted in S. W. Herman, Jr., *It's
> Your Souls We Want,* 3d ed., 1943, pp. 157-
> 58)

There was, thank God, much opposition to this
on the part of true Christian believers. But the
Nazis did succeed in many respects in twisting
Christian doctrine almost beyond recognition. A

church remained, but it was a church so badly confused with an atheistic state policy that the gospel virtually disappeared in official church life.

In Scripture, we have examples of what happens when this sort of thing takes place. In the Book of Acts we read (Acts 12:21-24):

> On an appointed day Herod put on his royal robes, took his seat upon the throne, and made an oration to them. And the people shouted, "The voice of a god, and not of man!" Immediately an angel of the Lord smote him, because he did not give God the glory; and he was eaten by worms and died. But the word of God grew and multiplied.

Just as God smote Herod on his throne for deifying himself to first-century Jews, so God smote Adolph Hitler in his bunker for making himself a god to the German people of the twentieth century. Truly, as Scripture says, "It is a fearful thing to fall into the hands of the living God."

Church history, then, shows us at least four dreadful misconceptions of the nature of the church and of the nature of Christianity. In Luther's day: Sacramentalism—making the church an end in itself. In Napoleon's day: Rationalism—setting Reason above the Word of God and turning the church into a rational institution, like a college of mathematicians. In Kierkegaard's day: Orthodoxism—substituting formal correctness of doctrine and the possession of Bibles for a living, personal encounter with Jesus Christ. And in Hitler's day: Politicism—blending the church with the state and allowing the culture of the time to swallow up the gospel of Christ.

* * *

But though we may recognize these errors historically, we generally overlook the fact that *they are also present in our own time,* and that *we ourselves commit them too.* No age begins without inheriting a great deal from the past, and the potential inheritance is both good and bad. Thus each of us must be very careful in his own life constantly to put his ideas under the searchlight of God's Word, so that he accepts from the past only what God would have him receive.

Several years ago, when I was at a conference in Toronto and was wearing clerical garb while walking down the street with some friends, a gentleman, obviously under the influence of alcohol, weaved towards us; as he passed he said to me in a thick voice: "Father, pray for me." Of course he thought I was a Roman Catholic priest, and he made me think of that poor fellow in the Martin Luther film who bought an indulgence, then went out and had a wild time of it and ended up in the gutter gripping his indulgence, which he regarded as his passport to heaven—"no confession necessary." This is the old sacramental error; but we had better not think that only Roman Catholics, Eastern Orthodox, and high Anglicans commit it! There are many members of evangelical Protestant churches who think that the pastor and the church somehow take care of the problem of salvation for them—that if they just remain in the church and attend services, something will happen in their behalf, whether they ever personally meet Christ or not. Indeed, they regard meeting Christ *as* simply sitting in the church and listening to its services. This is like confusing marriage with attending a wedding! In actuality, *meeting Christ consists of recognizing that MY sins sent Him to that Cross, that He died on that Cross in MY behalf, and that this very day He is willing and able to enter MY heart and reside there.* Sacramentalism isn't just in those places where incense and statues are used. The moral disease of Sacramentalism is present anywhere people get the idea that the church in itself has power to save—which, in fact, it *never* does. When a person thinks that the church saves, God meets him in judgment and not in grace, as we have emphasized before. *The same sun that melts the ice, hardens the clay. God never comes in neutrality.*

How about Rationalism today? We don't need to say much about this because Mr. High has said it for us without knowing it. There are many people in the church who are willing to play fast and loose with the Apostles' Creed and with other classic statements of Christian doctrine. Now I don't believe that the Apostles' Creed was inspired as was the Bible, but it is a much better creed than I could write myself, and I think that it is a much better creed than any theologians that I have ever met could write, and I'll wager that it is a much better creed than *you* could write. Moreover (and this is far more important), I am positive that the Apostles' Creed is absolutely validated by the Holy Scriptures, in the sense that it fully reflects central biblical teaching. The common tendency today to put ourselves above the creeds and even above the Scriptures is exceedingly dangerous. This doesn't mean that we cannot have problems and doubts; doubts are of the nature of faith, as Paul Tillich reminds us. The man who has no doubts, doesn't believe, for the starting point for all true Christian belief is the recognition of our finitude: "I believe; Lord, help my unbelief." It is one thing to have a doubt and to clear it up by faithful study of God's Word; it is another thing entirely to look at the Christian faith in such a way that I become a kind of god standing over it and criticizing it. Many people today—to their spiritual ruin—discard portions of the Creed and portions of the Scripture, and thereby come to worship their own supposedly rational faculties instead of the Father of our Lord Jesus Christ.

Now as to Orthodoxism in the contemporary scene. If it were possible, I would try to determine how many in my present audience read their Bibles every day. I certainly would like to know on the average how many church people read their Bibles daily. For many people, the only Bible they know consists of those sections of the Bible which appear in the Sunday morning service, and since not a few manage to sleep through the reading of those portions, very little of the Word of God comes to them. Perhaps this is one reason for the besetting sin of acting as though right doctrine automatically means meeting Christ. Let me tell you that there is no better theologian than the devil himself. The devil knows more theology than you or I ever will. Theology as such has never saved man and it never will, and a formal belief that the Bible is the Word of God has never saved a man and it never will. Salvation comes when, by way of personal contact with the Scriptures, we *personally meet the Christ of the Scriptures,* who loved us and gave himself for us.

Politicism? Well obviously there is no problem here, we say—not in Canada. Maybe in the Soviet Union and in China, but not here. However, listen to a sad tale. I recall a university chapel speaker—one of the most noted preachers in Canada—whose sermonic theme was as follows: "God became flesh; God entered the human situation; God got involved in human affairs. We as Christians must therefore get involved in human affairs, and particularly in economics. Canada has not captured the world markets for her industry, and what Canadian Christians have got to do is to enter into the economic sphere and bring about a situation whereby Canada does successfully gain the world markets for her industries." It took all the self-restraint I had not to walk out of that particular chapel talk, but somehow I managed it. It is unfortunate that I am a Lutheran, because if I were a Roman Catholic I am sure I would have received purgatorial credit for having sat through such a presentation! That chapel message was, however, especially interesting to me as an American citizen. Knowing that I am a U.S. citizen, Canadians have often said to me: "What is the matter with the United States? Down there, people think that the U.S. and the gospel are practically the same thing—that if the U.S. goes out and manages to bring American industry and Coca Cola to the Ubangi, this is practically the same thing as the gospel's reaching them. People in the United States are always confusing 'the American way of life' with Christianity." I grant that this criticism has a lot to it. And for this very reason it was very interesting to me to hear a Canadian churchman horribly confuse the gospel with Canada's economic life. I don't think that his remarks differed in principle from the Nazis' confusing the gospel with blood and soil and the Third Reich. Indeed, I think that the distance between the two is so slight that the one could actually slip into the other—into the spectre of the Religion of Nationalism. Fortunately, this speaker was an exception; but that chapel address should remind us of how easily the citizens of any country can reduce Christ's gospel to parochial national policy.

* * *

So we too are subject to the errors of the past. But the problem cuts deeper. We of the latter half of the twentieth century have contributed our own special misconceptions of the church's task. I think Mr. High has helped us to see some of the ways in which we, particularly, misunderstand the nature of the church. To be specific, we have, *inter alia,* contributed ACTIVISM to the ecclesiological misunderstandings of our forefathers. Many of us have the idea that if we leap about "doing good" we are bringing in the Kingdom of God. But in point of fact we may be doing no more than leaping about! There is a tendency in today's churches to engage in a great deal of this hyperactivism: constant attendance at meetings, never missing the spaghetti supper, the men's brotherhood, the ladies' aid, the ladies' sewing circle, etc. And this reflects on the pastor's problems. I have known pastors who have become absolutely exhausted just going from one meeting to another to begin the meetings with prayer. The feeling seems to be that opening prayer is invalid unless the pastor performs it. (Note the reappearance here of sacramentalism: "Father, pray for me," "Father, come to the meeting and lead the ladies' sewing circle in prayer"—so *I* won't have to do it.)

Every man is a priest before God, and if we would not place as much emphasis on meetings and activities and put more stress on the purpose of the church as we saw it in chapter two (the preaching of the gospel to every creature—to those who don't know Christ), we would be doing the church and its Lord a much greater service. I find no passage in the Bible which insists that there must be sewing bees in the church—or even spaghetti suppers. There are many activities carried on in the church today which are optional as far as the Bible is concerned. They are not wrong in themselves, but they can easily become wrong because they divert the energies of Christians from preaching the gospel.

Then we of the late twentieth century contribute to the falsifying of the church's proper function through our SUBJECTIVISM. Our time is possibly the most subjective period in all of church history. Today everybody talks in psychological terms. We enjoy nothing better than to probe our inner life and its real or imagined frustrations. We wallow in our misery. We go to psychologists, we go to psychiatrists, we go to counsellors. This predilection has been called "navel watching" by some people; that is to say, we enjoy nothing better than to sit down narcissistically and look at our own psychic navels. This delightful activity allows us to become completely involved in ourselves. We enjoy our problems. Someone has called our epoch "the Age of Analysis" (with reference particularly to psychoanalysis), and it *is* that, for we want to solve all our problems by subjective concentration on them. Luther, in diametric opposition to hypersubjectivism, says: "Christianity in its entirety lies outside us: in the righteousness of Christ and in the mercy of God" (*WA*, 25, 279— on Isa. 43:7). The man who has spiritual problems will never solve those problems by looking in upon himself. There is no solution inside; rather, the solution is outside. The solution lies in what God did for us on the Cross, and that depends not upon ourselves, but only upon the Christ who, "while we were yet sinners, died for us."

Also, our era is a period of TOGETHERNESS. There is nothing that we love to do more than to rub noses with each other. We just love to get folksy. Some people even cite in defense of this a theological term—*koinonia*. *Koinonia*, let it be understood, is a legitimate biblical term meaning "fellowship." And the Christian church, throughout its whole history, has experienced wonderful fellowship. Nobody denies this, but it is often forgotten that fellowship in the true biblical sense comes as a *by-product;* it is never a proper goal of the church. Fellowship comes because of the unity created by a single Lord, and because of a singleminded purpose to preach that Lord's Word. If you are fortunate enough to be in a church where the main emphasis is on preaching the gospel, where Christ is the center, then you know what real fellowship is—and it comes about not because you like the person who sits next to you in church, but because you see Christ in that person, whether he is white or black, whether he has halitosis or uses Sen-Sen!

It is very significant, I think, that in the New Testament there are no instances whatever of one apostle saying of another apostle, "My, I like him; he has the nicest personal characteristics." There was obviously wonderful fellowship in the New Testament church, but the fellowship came as a by-product, because the church focused its attention on Jesus Christ. When fellowship was lost, it was lost not because of a lack of togetherness, of social contact, but because of a lack of focus upon Jesus

Christ. Paul's problems with the Corinthians, for example, came about because they had gotten to the point where they couldn't even see Christ in the Lord's Supper. That's where they lost their sense of community. It was *not* because they didn't have enough meetings—or enough programs devoted to "fellowship"! The church today would do well to look very closely at itself in light of the negative example provided by Corinth.

Finally, we have contributed to the church's misunderstanding of herself by overweening contemporary ECUMENICALISM. Today, everybody gets excited about the u n i o n of church organizations and the formation of bigger churches. I suggest to you that there is no merit, necessarily, in churches coming together to make bigger churches. In some cases the result is simply greater inefficiency and a reduction of the effectiveness with which the gospel is preached, because the bigger an organization becomes, very often the less efficient it becomes. This has been set down effectively in humorous terms by an economist named Parkinson. Parkinson's "first law" is this: work expands to cover the number of people doing it. What this means is that if you hire thirteen secretaries in your office instead of the present three secretaries, the work will—amazingly—expand to the point where all thirteen secretaries are able to work all day long (or seem to do so) on what only three secretaries were able to do previously. There are plenty of examples which bear out this clever insight into human nature. In the United

States the WPA (the Works Progress Administration) provided a textbook illustration: during the great Depression of the thirties, the WPA made it possible for almost any number of people to lean on shovels and engage in apparently constructive activity. Work has a strange way of expanding to fit the number of people who are engaged in it. When I was the librarian of the University of Chicago Divinity School and had a staff of a dozen people, it was quite remarkable that with a reasonably stable amount of work to do, no matter how I expanded the staff, everybody still engaged in as much busy work as before—or so it seemed.

There is a tendency in the church to feel that by getting bigger we necessarily accomplish something. But there is nothing in the New Testament about increasing the size of an organization. There is a great deal about becoming one in Jesus Christ, but the oneness in Jesus Christ is the oneness of the SPIRIT, which may be reflected in the oneness of organization but need not be expressed in this way. We get wonderfully excited about the *fact* that large denominations are joining together today. I think we ought to be much more concerned about the *basis* on which they organize. Luther said, and we ought to ponder his words carefully: "Great numbers do not make the church. . . . We must look to the Word alone and judge on the basis of *that*" (WA, 42, 334). Are we judging ecumenicalism on the basis of the Word? When we do so, we find our emphasis shifting from church organizations to the innumerable unchurched people who desperately need Christ's saving gospel in our modern world.

* * *

We have talked about eight problems characteristic of the church's attitude toward herself: eight ways of misconstruing the nature of the church. Four have come from the past, and four are largely the products of our own time. We talked about the Sacramentalism, the Rationalism, the Orthodoxism, and the Politicism of earlier times and of our particular era; and we discussed the Activism, the Subjectivism, the Togetherness, and the Ecumenicalism of the mid-twentieth century. These are some of the major ways in which people have misunderstood, and continue to misunderstand, what the church really is.

In our final chapter we are going to see what answers God has in His grace provided for the kinds of problems we have encountered. I am absolutely convinced that until a person is aware of the problems it does no good—in fact it does genuine harm—to present solutions. A physician who arrives in your home and tries to stuff medicine down your gullet when you are not convinced that you have an illness is likely to do more harm than good. The same is equally true in the religious life. As Luther put it, until you understand the Law, that is, until you understand God's absolute demands and how far you fall short, you do not understand His Grace. Or as our Lord himself said of unbelievers: "If I had not come and spoken unto them, they would not have had sin" (Jn. 15:22, 24). Until the people of Jesus' day met the Law and the Gospel in Him, they did not really understand what sin was all about, and only when they understood sin could they understand how much it cost God to give His life to save them from it.

CHAPTER FOUR

"What Must I Do To Be Saved?"

Let us begin our final chapter with a word of prayer.

Dear God, our heavenly Father, we thank Thee for the insights and the help which we have received. We pray for the courage to be fully honest before Thee. We ask that Thou wouldst speak to our individual spiritual needs, whatever they are. We ask all these things in Jesus' name. Amen.

This is not going to be a long chapter. I am going to quote a passage of Scripture; I am going to make several remarks; and I am going to conclude with another passage of Scripture. I think that by way of these passages and by way of the remarks we will be able to see beyond the difficulties that have been described in our preceding chapters. I have intentionally taken you through the valley of the shadow of death in the previous sections. I have tried to show you where some very, very serious problems exist in our understanding of the church. Now that we have confronted these problems squarely, we are in a position to appreciate God's solution for them.

Our first Scripture reading is found in Matthew 19:16-26:

> And, behold, one came and said unto him, Good Master, what good thing shall I do, that I may have eternal life? And he said unto him, Why callest thou me good? There is none good but one, that is, God: but if thou wilt enter into life, keep the commandments. He saith unto him, Which? Jesus said, Thou shalt do no murder, Thou shalt not commit adultery, Thou shalt not steal, Thou shalt not bear false witness. Honour thy father and thy mother: and, Thou shalt love thy neighbour as thyself. The young man saith unto him, All these things have I kept from my youth up: what lack I yet? Jesus said unto him, If thou wilt be perfect, go and sell that thou hast, and give to the poor, and thou shalt have treasure in heaven: and come and follow me. But when the young man heard that saying, he went away sorrowful: for he had great possessions. Then said Jesus unto his disciples, Verily I say unto you, That a rich man shall hardly enter into the kingdom of heaven. And again I say unto you, It is easier for a camel to go through the eye of a needle, than for a rich man to enter into the kingdom of God. When his disciples heard it, they were exceedingly amazed, saying, Who then can be saved? But Jesus beheld them and said unto them, With men this is impossible; but with God all things are possible.

Notice that this "rich young ruler" claimed to have kept all of the commandments from his youth up; yet we know that no one has done this, for "all have sinned and come short of the glory of God" (Rom. 3:23). This man, in other words, did not recognize the extent of his need for God's grace. Instead of facing the real problem, he skirted the issue and asked, "What lack I yet?" Jesus replied: "If thou wilt be perfect" (which the man thought he was on the basis of the commandments), "go and sell that thou hast, and give to the poor, and thou shalt have treasure in heaven: and come and follow me." But "when the young man heard that saying, he went away sorrowful: for he had great possessions." Jesus, you see, drove the spike home in this man's life. He said, "Get rid of everything, and then come and follow me." This the man could not do, or would not do —thus making clear that he had *not* kept the commandments perfectly, for the essence of them is to "love the Lord your God *with all your heart."*

Then Jesus pointed out to his disciples how difficult it is for those whose hearts are set on their earthly possessions to enter the kingdom of heaven. And "when his disciples heard it, they were exceedingly amazed, saying, Who then can be saved?" It is very obvious from this that the disciples looked at the rich young ruler much as the man looked at himself: as an impeccable person, a person with power and influence, a person with background, a person of sterling morality. Yet this man refused Jesus' grace, and the disciples were stupefied. The disciples still thought of salvation in terms of the fulfilling of the Law by good works, whereas salvation can only come to those who stop relying upon their alleged "goodness," and instead accept God's grace in Jesus Christ. To the disciples' question, "Who then can be saved," Jesus answered: "With men this is impossible; but with God all things are possible," that is to say, what man cannot do in his weakness and sin, God can do through His power and grace in Christ.

In this book, we have confronted some staggering misconceptions in the church of the past and in the church of the present. We have seen greater men than any one of us fall. I doubt, for example, that any of us could write as literate and publishable an article on churchgoing as Stanley High's. None of us could write a book as witty, clever, and interesting as Thomas Paine's *Age of Reason.* "Who then can be saved?" "With men this is impossible; but with God all things are possible." Only by relying upon God's Word in Christ can we successfully deal with the numerous false views of the church which plague our time.

Thus we must go back to a proper conception of the church as we found it in Holy Scripture: the church as a divine institution created and sustained by God. The New Testament, as we have seen, regards the church as *separated from the world* (not a species of social club consisting of like-minded people), *God-centered* (not man-centered), *composed of "saints,"* that is, of people who recognize their absolute dependence upon God and need of Christ's sacrificial death for them; *and having as its central purpose the preaching of the gospel to every creature.* Now we shall see how this fourfold, revelationally based conception of the church, if adequately understood, can take care of the eight erroneous views we have talked about. Incidentally, it would be a very valuable experience for each of you, at your leisure, to reread Mr. High's article and see if you can correct it on the basis of the New Testament teaching about the church which has been presented here; if now you can say to yourself, "Aha, this is where I thought he was right, but now, on the basis of the New Testament, I can see where he isn't," then you will really have made progress in your understanding of the church and of your proper relation to it!

We said first of all that the church requires radical separation—that it is different from every other institution. If we know it is different then we won't commit the error which I called the "fellowship" error. We won't try to turn the church into a social club. We will see that the church, as distinct from a club, is a place where the gospel is preached. Then a very strange thing will happen: we will receive fellowship as a by-product! "Seek ye first the kingdom of God and His righteousness, and all these things shall be added unto you," said Jesus in the Sermon on the Mount. The man who seeks as an end something which is properly only a by-product, gains nothing at all. But the person who seeks the proper end gains by-products as well. Moreover, if we see the church as something different from human organizations in the world, we will be unlikely to make the mistake of many advocates of "ecumenicalism"—the mistake of thinking that just to make a church bigger is to make it better. Often we think of the church much as we think of a business corporation or a farm, and we want to make it bigger, always bigger, by absorbing smaller units or by mergers. But "great numbers," as Luther says, "do *not* make the church"—indeed, they have nothing at all to do with the nature of the church. The church is something different; it is the place where God meets man through Word and Sacrament.

Then we pointed out the radical God-centeredness of the church. If the church to us is a God-centered institution, not a man-centered one—if the main concern in the church is with God and not with you and me personally—then we will not run into the difficulties of "Rationalism" and "Orthodoxism." A person becomes a rationalist when he sets himself in the center and God on the periphery. Such a man thinks that his own reason is so important that it can determine what portions of the Bible to accept, or what parts of the Creed to accept; but the man who places God in the center is a person like Luther, who said of the great mystery of the Trinity, "I can only doff my hat and go my way." And the God-centered person or the God-centered congregation is not going to fall into the error of "Orthodoxism," for the true believer knows that the living God never permits himself to be put into the pocket, closed up, manipulated. If we look at the church in terms of ourselves— with us in the center—then before long we think that we own the Word of God and can say the last word about it; but if we look at the church as having God as its center, then *He* speaks through the Word, and we must remove our shoes and listen.

We spoke, thirdly, about the church as the place where men hear God's call and become "saints," that is, people declared holy because of what Christ has done for them on the Cross. If this is our conception of the church, then we won't become "Sacramentalists," for we won't think there is something *automatically* good in going to the Lord's Table, or in joining the ladies' aid, or even in being a church member. We will see that the essence of the church rests in God's call and in Christ's death on the Cross—and these are *never* automatic. You can't even use a mechanical term such as "automatic" to describe those hours Jesus spent on the Cross pouring out His life's blood, not because He had to but because He wanted to. This is not automatic; this is not the work of a machine. Rather, this is the work of a Person—the God of Love. "For a good man, one might dare to die," says Saint Paul, "but while we were yet sinners, Christ died for us." Furthermore, this conception of the church as the congregation of saints prevents the "Activistic" error. The Activist thinks that by what *we* do the church comes into being—that the more spaghetti suppers per month, the better the church is. But what has "being declared holy," "being made a saint" through Christ's saving work, got to do with spaghetti and "busyness"? A proper New Testament conception of the church will remind us not of Martha, who was "cumbered about much serving," but of Mary, who "sat at Jesus' feet and heard His word."

And if we realize the central purpose of the church, that it is to preach the gospel to every creature, then we will not slip into the errors of "Politicism" and "Subjectivism." When the preaching of Christ's gospel means more to us than anything else in the church, we will not allow the markets of Canada, or the Coca Cola company, or the Third Reich, or any other political or cultural factor, to become confused with the nature of the church, for the gospel is totally different from all such things. They are of earth; the gospel is the God-provided link with eternity. And if the preaching of the gospel is our highest value, we will not spend our time in church introspectively gazing at our own problems, concentrating on our own difficulties. Instead, we will look to Christ, the One on whom the entire gospel focuses, and we will be so concerned about those outside the church who have never met Him that we won't have time to worry about our subjective difficulties.

Let me give a personal example. Once, when I was a very young Christian and very concerned with "the inner life," I went to a Christian bookstore for literature on the subject. The owner of this Christian bookstore was away, but his wife was there. I asked her for works of a somewhat subjectivistic character, and she said: "My husband has gotten a few of these books for the bookstore but we don't push them particularly. He says that if people would worry more about

those who don't know Christ, they wouldn't have
time to read this kind of thing." That really
struck me; I realized how much time I had spent
in inner probing instead of getting out and seeing
what the church is to do to reach the lost in our
age. Certainly works such as Norman Vincent
Peale's *Power of Positive Thinking* can provide
some help in the Christian life. But the great
saints of God I've known have not had much time
to read these books. The Cross is too important.
I just can't imagine St. Paul in the desert reading
The Power of Positive Thinking. Subjectivism no
more than Politicism can survive the New Testament view of the church with its overwhelming
stress upon "teaching all nations" concerning the
saving love of Christ.

* * *

Now for some concluding remarks of a rigor-
ously practical nature. You have every right to
ask: "What does all of this say to me?" Let me
point out some specifics. First: it has been my purpose here to make you ask yourself: What do I
think of the church? What is my conception of the
church? What is my idea of my own relationship
to God in the church? A person must begin at
this point, and one must be ruthlessly honest with
himself. If you find that you have fallen into some
of the misconceptions that we have discussed, then
be honest enough to admit it to yourself. It is not
important whether you admit it to me, but it is
desperately important that you see what is really
happening in your own life or in the life of your

congregation. To become aware of the problem is always the first step in solving it.

Then, secondly, it is essential that you see that the way out of this morass is *not* by deeper and deeper examinations of yourself, or by more and more detailed analyses of church history, or by talking at great length to other people about the difficulties of the church. The only way out is TO SHIFT YOUR ATTENTION FROM THE PROBLEM TO CHRIST. "With *God* all things are possible." God's salvation is a sure thing because it does not depend upon us. If you see that you have misunderstood the nature of the church, then only by turning to Christ and finding the answer in Him can you experience any real assurance. The more you look into yourself, the more lack of assurance you will have. The man who concentrates upon himself loses everything. "Whosoever will save his life shall lose it," said Christ, "but whosoever will lose his life for My sake shall find it." The man who loses his life for Christ's sake, the man who moves his attention from himself to Christ—this is the man who receives salvation, and salvation is absolutely assured for the person who relies on Jesus Christ as the center of his life. I like Paul Tillich's definition of faith as "ultimate concern." This means that everybody has faith and there are no atheists, for everyone has *something* that means more to him than anything else. The question then is: What is *your* ultimate concern? Be honest with yourself. What is the ultimate concern in your life? What is the last thing you would give up?

To see the church correctly, to see one's relationship with God correctly, necessitates having *Christ* as one's ultimate concern—as the focal point of one's entire existence.

The natural reaction to this is to say: "I realize that Christ should be at the very center of my life, but the concerns of business or the family invariably move into the center and Christ is displaced to a subordinate position. This happens again and again in my life." The trouble here is that we forget that faith is a moment-by-moment experience with God and that faith does not come out of the blue. You don't get faith by sitting down and trying to "work it up" viscerally. You can huff and you can puff but faith does not come. In the Scripture we are told that "faith comes by hearing and hearing by the Word of God" (Rom. 10:17). Faith is God's gift, and He gives it through His Word. I suggest to you, therefore, that if you have difficulty in keeping Christ at the center of your life, run (not walk!) to a Christian bookstore, and there buy a pocket-sized Bible to keep close to you every moment of your life. Take it with you to your job and each day let God speak to you *frequently* through it. Read especially the New Testament, for the New Testament fulfills the Old. Make the Gospel of John your favorite book, as it was Luther's; there God's saving message is presented again and again and again—with maximum clarity and simplicity.

And don't tell yourself that you can't maintain such daily contact with God's Word! You know very

well that every day you take any number of cof-
fee breaks (call them what you will); you can just
as easily take "spiritual breaks"—and these are
far more essential, for "faith comes by hearing
and hearing by the Word of God." If you want to
have the kind of vital faith that we have been
talking about, you must keep yourself in contact
with the means that God has provided to bring
this faith to you.

"But," I can hear some disgruntled voice
saying, "you haven't spent any time at all on
the ethical and moral regulations for the Christian life. I go to my job and you haven't done
anything to help me solve my particular ethical
problems. What do I do when there is a moral
question as to the proper treatment of my business
associates or employees, etc., etc? What do I
do?" I haven't the faintest idea what you should
do, and I would not presume to give you advice.
What I do know is this: If the gospel remains in
the center of your life, and if your ultimate concern is the Cross of Christ, then God through His
Holy Spirit and Word will guide you dynamically
to make your unique decisions in accordance with
His grace. The great medieval church father
Augustine once advised: "Love God, and do as you
please." If we love God in the biblical sense, only
what pleases Him will be pleasing to us.

There is no way to state ahead of time how to
solve the multifarious problems of the Christian
life. Your life is unique, my life is unique, and it
is only by living close to Christ that you and I can

make our decisions in accordance with God's will. I could of course, provide you with hypothetical solutions to any number of hypothetical difficulties; but you would discover that all the problems were included except yours! There is no comprehensive set of laws that can take care of you in the Christian life, any more than there is any comprehensive set of rules that can tell you how to live a happily married life. We are not saved by law; we are saved by grace—by the grace that brings the Holy Spirit to us. It is He who works in our hearts to guide us in making daily decisions in accordance with God's will as revealed in Holy Writ.

The religion of the New Testament is a dynamic living faith which comes about because Christ lives dynamically in the heart. Living ethically is for the Christian only another by-product. If you are terribly worried about ethics, if you concentrate on ethics as the be-all and end-all, you are going to miss not only the Christian faith, but true ethics as well! But if you stick to Christ and make Him your ultimate concern, the ethical will take care of itself. Love God, and do as you please.

* * *

We now come to our final Scripture passage— Rev. 3:14-22. This passage could be taken as the text of my entire book. (Had I given the text at the outset of these chapters—some people would immediately have fallen asleep, convinced that they knew how it was going to be developed. So first I gave the presentation, and *now* I supply the text!) I think it will now be quite plain in what way this can be regarded as the text for everything we have said:

> And unto the angel of the church of the Laodiceans write; These things saith the Amen, the faithful and true witness, the beginning of the creation of God; I know thy works, that thou art neither cold nor hot: I would thou wert cold or hot. So then, because thou art lukewarm, and neither cold nor hot, I will spue thee out of my mouth. Because thou sayest, I am rich, and increased with goods, and have need of nothing; and knowest not that thou art wretched, and miserable, and poor, and blind, and naked: I counsel thee to buy of me gold tried in the fire, that thou mayest be rich; and white raiment, that thou mayest be clothed, and that the shame of thy nakedness do not appear; and anoint thine eyes with eyesalve, that thou mayest see. As many as I love, I rebuke and chasten: be zealous therefore, and repent. Behold, I stand at the door, and knock: if any man hear my voice, and open the door, I will come in to him, and will sup with him, and he with me. To him that overcometh will I grant to sit with me in my throne, even as I also overcame, and am set down with my Father in his throne. He that hath an ear, let him hear what the Spirit saith unto the churches.

The church of the Laodiceans is the church of our day, a church that is neither cold nor hot, and God actually prefers the cold to the lukewarm! The church of our time must recognize that it is "wretched, miserable, poor, blind, and naked," because it has an inflated conception of its own importance. And our church—and this means every one of us personally—must go to Christ and obtain of Him the true riches that flow from His love. This means nothing less than personal recognition of how badly we have perverted Christ's body, the church—and it means throwing open the door to the Christ who stands seeking entrance to the church He redeemed with His own blood.

Damnation through the church is possible only when one is indifferent to or rejects the grace of God. Christ stands without the door of your heart. You can, and will, be "damned through the church" if you insist on keeping that door shut either because you refuse to hear the knocking, or because you regard other things as more important. But if you will open the door, He will come in and will sup with you and this will be the fulfillment of your life. Then one day, He promises, you will sit with Him on His throne, even as He sits at the right hand of the Father. With God all things are possible. Amen.

SCRIPTURE INDEX

INDEX